COASTERS OF
THE AVON AND SEVERN

by
Bernard McCall

INTRODUCTION

The origins of this book lie with the publication of *Coasters around Britain* in 1989. That book looked at coasters in a wide variety of small ports throughout the United Kingdom, and I felt at the time that it should be followed up by a series of books looking in more detail at shipping activity in some areas. *Coasters of the Avon and Severn* is the first book in this series. Hopefully it will be followed by other similar books looking at coasters in specific areas, and not only in the UK.

Since I began to publish the bi-monthly magazine *Coastal Shipping* in 1994, it has become clear that there is a vast amount of excellent photographic material which deserves to be shared with a wider audience. Again, this series will allow such photographs to be appreciated. All photographers have been credited beneath their photographs and I thank them for making their precious images available for this book.

Much thought has been given to the most suitable format for the series and I have decided on A5 landscape format for several reasons. Firstly, it allows a good-sized photograph to be accompanied by a caption while keeping production costs to a minimum and therefore allowing purchasers to build up a set of all books in the series at reasonable cost. Secondly, it continues the successful format used for *Coastal Shipping* magazine.

The photographs in the book cover a period of forty years. There is no doubt that shipping activity on the Avon and Severn has changed dramatically in that time. With only very occasional calls by coasters to Bristol's City Docks and to Gloucester, the maritime centres of these fine cities have been devoted to "redevelopment" - and all that that entails. One cannot hold back the march of time, but it is sometimes difficult to call it progress especially when one looks at some of the so-called redevelopment schemes. Furthermore, there must surely be sound economic and environmental arguments for restoring commercial traffic to the Sharpness - Gloucester Canal.

For those who wish to wallow in nostalgia and remember coastal shipping as it used to be, I hope that this book will make that possible. A brief history of each ship has been included in the captions to allow enthusiasts to view the main outline of each vessel's career and possibly recall her under a different name. These histories are certainly not exhaustive, and they do not include tonnage figures. Such details would reduce the appeal of the book to more general readers. As far as possible, the ship's histories have been corrected up to the end of 1998.

Bernard McCall   Portishead, March 1999

ACKNOWLEDGEMENTS

As noted above, the first vote of thanks must go to those photographers who have loaned their material for this book. Many of them have also provided help with captions for the photographs. It was the work of Cedric Catt which first inspired this book. Other individuals must be thanked, notably Gil Mayes who has checked many of the details in the book. Specific queries have been answered by Captain Peter Herbert, Mr M T Winter and Dr Jürgen Ehlers. Redcliffe Professional Colour Laboratories are thanked for the printing of original colour prints. If there are any errors, they are all mine and I apologise in advance for them! I also wish to thank the staff of Astec Printers.

There are several publications which have provided inspiration and information. Specific mention should be made of the following : *The Golden Harvest* by P Gosson and R Parsons; *Bristol Seaport* by Colin Momber; *Bristol City Docks* by P W Hobday; *The Floating Harbour* by J Lord and J Southam; *Gloucester Docks* by Hugh Conway-Jones. Details of the ships' histories could not have been compiled without recourse to *Lloyd's Register of Shipping* and *Marine News* (the monthly journal of the World Ship Society). Any readers wishing to learn more about coasters and the trades in which they work should subscribe to the author's bi-monthly magazine *Coastal Shipping*.

One of the best vantage points for observing shipping approaching the Rivers Avon and Severn is Battery Point at Portishead where the main shipping channel passes close inshore. A seafront promenade and grassy embankment make ship watching an enjoyable activity - at least in fine weather. Ships can sail by during a period covering some four hours before high water and two hours after. On 27 February 1999, the *Sociality* passes Battery Point and heads for Avonmouth at the end of a voyage from Wicklow. At a time when the British connections of UK coastal shipping grow ever slimmer, she offers many reminders of the heyday of such shipping in years gone by. She was built in 1986 by Cochrane Shipbuilders Ltd, of Selby, for J Wharton (Shipping) Ltd, based on the River Trent. The Cochrane yard is closed and the Wharton company no longer owns ships. After less than a year under the Wharton name of *Stevonia*, she was transferred to the ownership of F T Everard Shipping Ltd in early 1987 and took the Everard name of *Sociality*. Thankfully, this company lives on as a major British owner and operator of coastal vessels.

(Bernard McCall)

3

It is a warm, spring Saturday and Battery Point attracts visitors who mainly come to stroll but who are still keen to observe the passing ships. On 13 March 1999, they were rewarded with ten shipping movements which included the departure of the tanker *Anchorman* and the sand dredger *Welsh Piper*. The *Anchorman* was built in Johore by the Malaysia Shipyard and has a name associated with traditional British tanker owners Rowbotham Tankships Ltd. This company was taken over by P & O, and management of the fleet passed to P & O Tankships Ltd. In late 1996, it was announced that P & O had sold the tankers to James Fisher and Sons plc. The *Anchorman* is owned by a Liberian-flag company and is bareboat chartered to James Fisher Tankships Ltd. With the Bristol Channel providing a rich source of sand and aggregates, dredgers have been a frequent sight at ports on both sides of the Channel and several will be seen in the pages of this book. The *Welsh Piper*, built at Appledore in 1987, represents a significant development in the local fleet for she was the first self-discharging dredger to be built for the Bristol Channel.

(Bernard McCall)

4

On the south side of the Bristol Channel and west of the mouth of the River Avon lies Portishead dock, opened in 1879 but now closed to commercial traffic. This splendid view from 1957/58 shows Portishead B power station under construction. Passing the pier outward bound is the **Brandon** built locally by Charles Hill & Sons Ltd in 1957 and owned locally by Osborn and Wallis. Like her fleetmate **Colston** (see page 51), she was a regular visitor to Portishead with coal for the power station. Leaving the dock are two further Osborn and Wallis vessels - the **Salcombe** and the **St Vincent**. The **Salcombe** was built at Lekkerkerk in 1938 as **Camroux IV** and was renamed **Salcombe** in 1942. The **St Vincent**, however, was built at Hill's Bristol yard in 1940. She left the British flag in 1969 when sold to Greek owners who renamed her **Giankaros II**. She suffered an ignominious end for Italian coastguards discovered her carrying contraband cigarettes and hashish but her crew set fire to her and she later sank. The **Salcombe** also left the fleet in 1969 and was bought by British owner G Dupenois Shpg Co Ltd and renamed **Friars Craig**. She sailed out to the West Indies, but was eventually laid up at Bridgetown, Barbados, with crankshaft damage. After a decade thus laid up, all useful gear was removed and she was sunk as a wreck for divers off Barbados. By the late 1980s, the **Brandon** had been sold to other owners on at least two occasions but had kept her original name. In July 1987, when on passage from Casablanca to Houston, she suffered engine trouble and was towed to Lisbon. Laid up and later arrested there, she was eventually scrapped locally in late 1989.   (M T Winter collection)

Just entering the mouth of the River Avon, the Bristol Steam Navigation Company's **Milo** heads back to her home port on 11 March 1954 after undergoing trials in the Bristol Channel. She had, of course, been built in the city at the Charles Hill yard. A notable feature of her design was the integration of funnel and bridge. Sold to Glasgow owners J & A Gardner Ltd in 1969, she was renamed **Saint Angus**. She suffered a serious fire on 21 July 1975 but was repaired by Tyne Dock Engineering Co Ltd. In 1976, she was sold to Maldive Island owners and was renamed **Lady Maria**. Her new career proved to be very brief for she was declared a total loss after grounding on the Somali coast on 18 August 1976.

(Philip Hoskins)

The **Western Coast** is seen underway in the River Avon and passing Sea Mills on 10 August 1953. Coast Lines vessels were regular visitors to the City Docks. The **Western Coast**, built by the Goole Shipbuilding and Repair Company, was just two years old when this photograph was taken. In 1958, she was transferred within the Coast Lines group to William Sloan and was renamed **Tay**. When she left the British flag in 1968, the selling company was noted as Burns and Laird Lines, again a constituent of the Coast Lines group. Her Panamanian purchasers renamed her **Charalambos** and she traded mainly in the Mediterranean for the next five years. Her sale to a Cypriot company in 1973 resulted in her being renamed **Erika** but her career soon ended while on passage from Galatz to, rather surprisingly, Hull. Sadly she never made it back to England for she struck a rock off Roubos Island on 14 May 1973. She grounded and subsequently sank in shallow water. *(Philip Hoskins)*

7

The ***Cornel*** was built by E J Smit & Zoon at Westerbroek in 1938 for Cardiff shipowners Lovering and Sons Ltd. Although based in Cardiff, this family company specialised in transporting coal from Point of Ayr colliery in North Wales and from small mines in the Forest of Dean. The ***Cornel*** called regularly at Lydney to load from the latter mines. After the Second World War, she traded more widely. This splendid photograph shows her outward bound from Bristol (John Lovering's birthplace, incidentally) in the River Avon on 7 April 1953. In 1958, she was sold to Thomas Rose and Co, of Sunderland, and was renamed ***Glenside***. She left the British flag in 1965 when she was bought by Greek owners for whom she traded as ***Michael A***, and a further sale within Greece ten years later led to her being renamed ***Elenitsa K***. She sank off the coast of Greece on 26 September 1983.

(*Philip Hoskins*)

The Cypriot-flagged **Sykron** is an example of the highly-successful Type 58 vessels built by the prolific J J Sietas yard on the outskirts of Hamburg. She was delivered to her original owners on 4 September 1970 and was named **Julia**. Subsequent name changes saw her become **Anna H** in 1985, **Chezine** in 1987, **Sykron** in 1990 and finally **Amavisti** in May 1996. She is one of a sub-group within the class having an extra wheelhouse built into the funnel. This feature, which coincidentally echoes a similar idea seen on the **Milo** on page 6, allowed an extra tier of containers to be carried on deck without impairing forward vision. However it was not containers she was heading to Bristol to load on 15 March 1992, but rather heavy lifts. As another coaster had arrived the previous day, there was an unusual opportunity to see two coasters together in the Cumberland Basin.

(Bernard McCall)

The date is 19 July 1953 and the sun shines brightly as the *Arklow*, owned by the Clyde Shipping Company, heads up the River Avon and passes beneath the Clifton suspension bridge. Built at Kalmar, Sweden, in 1948 as the *Westhor*, she became *Frosti* in 1950, a name which reflected her ability to carry refrigerated cargoes. It was in 1952 that she was sold to Clyde Shipping and renamed *Arklow*, a name which she kept for five years but she was then sold on in 1957 and was renamed *San Martin*. A further change of ownership in 1964 saw her renamed, again appropriately, *Glacier*. In 1966, she was renamed *Ross Eastern Leader* and this would appear to suggest the start of a new career as a fishing vessel. Her name was changed to *Tjamar* in 1971 and it seems that she still works as such, now flying the Panamanian flag, though it is unknown where she is presently based.

(Philip Hoskins)

Elsewhere in this book will be found photographs of several of the sand dredgers which have loaded cargoes in the Bristol Channel and delivered them to Bristol. In the early 1990s, deliveries to the City Docks were coming to an end but this period saw the use of the largest dredger to sail up the Avon, the **Arco Scheldt**, whose considerable bulk should be compared to sand dredgers found on other pages. Built by Appledore Shipbuilders in 1972, she began life as **Amey III** but was renamed **Arco Scheldt** in 1973. Owned by ARC Marine Ltd, this company took over the family-owned Holms Sand & Gravel Co Ltd in 1987. Its vessels are still a common sight in the Bristol Channel, though discharge of cargoes is now effected at Avonmouth rather than Bristol. The **Arco Scheldt**, seen arriving at Bristol on 14 June 1990, was sold for demolition in Belgium in March 1997.

(Bernard McCall)

As noted on page 9, coasters do continue to sail up the River Avon to the City Docks to load heavy lift cargoes manufactured near the docks. Brunel's magnificent suspension bridge at Clifton affords a fine view not only of the city but of river traffic. The **RMS Westfalia** is seen leaving the lock on 18 August 1994 to deliver two silos across the Bristol Channel to Barry. She was built at the Brake yard of C Lühring in 1980 as the **Atoll**. She kept this name until February 1993 when she was renamed **Karin E** and took her present name later in mid-June of that same year.

(Bernard McCall)

A busy scene in the Cumberland Basin on the fine evening of 23 June 1975. As the **Sand Gem** and **Sand Jade** enter the Basin from Hotwells, the loaded **Sand Opal**, **Harry Brown** and **Badminton** prepare to move into the City Docks. Dredgers from three different companies are represented in this picture. Sand Supplies (Western) Ltd discharged at Hotwells Dock and Renwick's Wharf; the Holms Sand and Gravel Company had wharves at the Grove and Bathurst Basin; and Bristol Dredging Ltd had its facilities at Pooles Wharf (Hotwells) and Redcliffe Street.

(Cedric Catt)

A real old-timer. The **Colon** was built in 1919 by H and C Grayson, of Liverpool. Owned by MacAndrews, whose vessels were frequent callers to the City Docks with cargoes of oranges from Seville, she was very nearly at the end of her life when she was photographed in the Cumberland Basin on 30 March 1954. In fact, during June 1954 she was sold to the British Iron and Steel Company for demolition and was allocated to Smith and Houston. She arrived at Port Glasgow on 9 July 1954. In these days of frequent name changes for ships, it is worth noting that she kept the same name throughout her life.

(Philip Hoskins)

Despite the most careful calculations, there are occasions when all does not go according to plan when a ship is being launched. Charles Hill's shipyard built the **Dido** for the Bristol Steam Navigation Co, and she was launched on 10 June 1963. However, this unusual photograph shows her remaining partly on the slipway an hour after her "launch". In 1977, she was bought by Liverpool shipowners Coe Metcalf Shipping Ltd and was renamed **Gorsethorn**. In 1990, she was sold and converted to a floating radio station named **Déesse de la Democratie** ("Goddess of Democracy")

(P W Hobday)

The mini-bulker **Moidart** was owned by Milton Shipping Co Ltd and managed by Denholm Maclay Co Ltd, of Glasgow. She moves forward to turn in the City Docks on 6 April 1977 following repairs at the Albion Dockyard. She left Bristol on the evening tide of the same day. In the drydock is the **Silver Cloud**, more details of which will be found on page 33. The **Moidart** was built at the well-known yard of E J Smit & Zoon, Westerbroek, in 1972. She was sold and renamed **Adriatic** in 1986 and two years later was sold again and renamed **Leo**. Under that name she continues to trade under the Maltese flag for Bennar Shipping Co Ltd.

(Cedric Catt)

The **Sand Pearl**, operated by Sand Supplies (Western) Ltd and inward bound to deliver a cargo to Renwicks Wharf, passes the company's newly-acquired **Frierfjord** at Hotwells on 28 September 1979. The **Frierfjord** had recently arrived from Norway and was due to sail to Cardiff where she would undergo conversion to a sand dredger. She was built at Brattvåg, Norway, in 1973.

(Cedric Catt)

After sale and conversion, the **Frierfjord** was renamed **Sand Diamond** and she is seen here at Hotwells on 31 July 1980, newly converted from a mini bulk carrier to a sand dredger and ready for service in her new role. Beneath the overhead travelling crane, the **Sand Gem** is being discharged in Hotwells Dock. The **Sand Diamond** was sold to owners in the Middle East in 1992. She was renamed **Tariq** and continues to trade for the Alwardi Marine & Dredging Company, of Bahrain.

(Cedric Catt)

There was a steady trade in the export of coke from the gas works in the City Docks. Much of the coke was taken to Scandinavia and on 21 September 1964 we find the German *Gerlinde* loading for Denmark. Something of a veteran, she was launched at Boizenburg on the River Elbe in April 1912 and was completed on 27 July that year as an ocean-going barge. Originally named *Frieda*, she was converted to a motor cargo ship in May 1927. In 1951 she was renamed *Heike Schlüter*, and took the name *Gerlinde* in December 1957. The next sale in 1965 saw her change name to *Inge S*. The year 1973 proved to be an eventful one. Firstly she was sold to a Finnish owner and renamed *Inge* and later in the year, owners based in Famagusta, Cyprus, bought her and renamed her *Medina*. On 3 November 1973, she grounded near Ristma after springing a leak while on passage from Helsinki to Oskarshamn. She was abandoned by her crew and was declared a total loss.

(P W Hobday)

The carriage of timber in packaged form has long since meant the demise of loose timber, often stowed on deck in what now would be considered an inefficient way. The attractive Dutch coaster **Prosperite** was photographed at the berth known as F Site on 14 July 1965 as work begins to discharge her cargo of timber loaded at Mantyluoto in Finland. Typical of Dutch vessels dating from the 1950s, the **Prosperite** was built at the Slikkerveer yard of De Groot and Van Vliet in 1956. She was sold in 1970 to Greek owners in Thessaloniki and was renamed **Galini**. She served her Greek owner well for 22 years and was then sold on in 1990, being renamed **Kyparissia Th**, **Jamal** and **Kaptan Hasan** in quick succession. Her final renaming came in 1994 when she took the name **Jasemin S**. She sank in February of the following year. Just to the east of the F Site berth is home of the former German coaster **Thekla** which arrived in Bristol in 1983 and, now a floating night-club, is barely recognisable from her original appearance.

(P W Hobday)

19

Upstream of Avonmouth, Bristol Corporation had a berth on the north bank of the River Avon for the loading of effluent on to a tanker. The effluent was then disposed of far enough out in the Bristol Channel for there to be no pollution dangers. However, the 1990s saw increasing concern about ecological and environmental issues, and the disposal of effluent at sea was a casualty of legislation which reflected such concern. The *Glen Avon*, photographed at her berth on the Avon on 21 August 1988, was built in 1969 by the Ailsa shipyard at Troon. Although it would have been possible for her to work longer before the full implementation of legislation which would bring about the demise of such tankers at the end of 1998, her then owners, the Wessex Water Authority, decided to sell the *Glen Avon* in 1993. She was bought by a Nigerian company and was converted to a conventional tanker at Sharpness, being renamed *Olokun II*.   (Bernard McCall)

Before looking at shipping in Avonmouth Docks, we return momentarily to Battery Point at Portishead to see the passing of the **Neermoor** on her way to Avonmouth from Rochefort on 13 March 1999 to load ammonium nitrate. Owned in Germany but flying the flag of Antigua & Barbuda, she is one of an increasing number of coastal vessels built for western European owners by the Slovenske Lodenice shipyard at Komarno on the River Danube in Czechoslovakia. Her passing is being committed to film by a young enthusiast.

(Bernard McCall)

The **Einstein** is a Type 58 coaster from the prolific building yard of J J Sietas on the outskirts of Hamburg. Built in 1969, she was delivered to German owners on 8 August that year named **Bismarkstein**. Although renamed **Eland** in 1969 and **Elbestroom** in 1972, she reverted to her original name in 1975. Three years later, she became **Stephanie** but reverted yet again to **Bismarkstein** in 1980. She took the name **Einstein** in 1986 and has kept this name since then. In this view, dated 18 May 1998, she is arriving at Avonmouth to discharge a cargo of wheat from the German port of Neustadt.

(P W Hobday)

Vessels flying the flag of the Faroe Islands are not frequent callers at British ports. The **Nestindur**, however, was photographed leaving Avonmouth on 17 May 1985 after discharging a cargo of animal feed from Seville. She was built at Kalmar in Sweden as the **Frigg** in 1965, being renamed **Karen Wonsild** in 1970 and then **Nestindur** in 1974. In the year after this photograph was taken, she was sold to Panamanian flag operators and was renamed **Alaa M** and was sold on in 1990, this time to St Vincent flag owners who renamed her **Marineta**. Her end came after she grounded near Crotone, Italy, on 6 January 1993. She was abandoned by her crew after taking in water while on passage from Turkey to La Nouvelle in southern France, and she became a total loss.

(Cedric Catt)

We now move into Avonmouth Docks where oil and petroleum products have long contributed to the prosperity of the port. The Oil Basin in the docks was completed in 1921 and reconstructed in 1965. The **Acclivity** represents a style of coastal tanker from a much earlier generation. Seen in the Oil Dock on 29 March 1965, she was nearing the end of her working life. She had been built as the **Atheltarn** for the United Molasses Company, and took the name **Acclivity** following her sale to Everard Shipping Co Ltd in 1952. She was sold for demolition in Belgium in May 1966.

(P W Hobday)

During the 1990s, natural gas from small oil fields in the south of England has been exported through Avonmouth. Regular destinations include Ireland, Portugal and France. On 23 May 1995, the **Erik Kosan** loads 1400 tonnes of butane at No 2 Oil Jetty for delivery to Port Jerome on the River Seine. This tanker was built at Kristiansand S, Norway, in 1978 as the **Francis Drake** and became **Erik Tholstrup** in 1985 after purchase by Kosan Tankers. She took the name **Erik Kosan** in 1990. Late in 1998 when the oldest in the fleet of Lauritzen Kosan Tankers, this vessel was bareboat chartered for five years to Bunkerimg Services International Inc, with Transgas Shipping Line, of Lima, as managers. She is now used for coastal work in Peru. At the end of the charter, the vessel will be purchased by Transgas. On 2 December 1998, she was renamed **Virgo Gas 1** at Antwerp and left that port for Houston two days later.

(P W Hobday)

Vessels operated by the Cardiff based shipowning company Charles M Willie & Co are frequent callers at ports on the English side of the Bristol Channel. Their usual trading pattern sees them linking ports in the south-west of England to the Iberian peninsula. On 7 April 1997, the **Celtic Navigator** was discharging forest products at R Shed, Avonmouth. The cargo had been loaded at the Portuguese port of Leixoes. This coaster was one of a standard class of eight vessels built between 1974 and 1980 at the Barkmeijer Shipyard, Stroobos, in Holland. The penultimate vessel in the series, she was launched for Dutch owners as **Engel Klein** in 1979. She was renamed **Marant** in 1983, then **Wilant** in 1988. The latter name was shortlived, for she was purchased by her Welsh owners in 1989 and renamed **Celtic Navigator**. She currently sails under the flag of the Bahamas.

(P W Hobday)

The attractive setting of Battery Point at Portishead is seen to good advantage in this view of the container vessel **Christine O** on her way to Avonmouth at the end of a voyage from Waterford on 13 March 1999. She links the two ports, making two or three round trips across the Irish Sea each week. Built as the **John Bluhm** in 1978 by J J Sietas at Hamburg, she kept her original name until mid-November 1998 when she was renamed **Christine O**. She is a very useful multi-purpose vessel, being able to carry timber and general cargoes in addition to containers.

(Bernard McCall)

A spectacular scene in the Avon Gorge on 8 May 1976 as the loaded **Sand Jade**, moving slowly on the incoming tide, and the departing **HMS Crichton**, with fenders out, exchange greetings at very close quarters. **HMS Crichton** was followed a few minutes later by **HMS Repton**, both having been on a courtesy visit to Bristol City Docks.

(Cedric Catt)

An unusual visitor to Bristol on 17 September 1977 was the German coaster *Gaa*. She is seen berthed adjacent to the entrance lock of the Cumberland Basin, and is positioned over the grid iron. Once the tide has gone out, vessels lie on the grid, thus allowing rudder, propeller and hull to be examined without the need for drydocking. The *Gaa* was built in 1950 by Stader Schiffsw. at Stade as *Krautsand* and she was lengthened and deepened in 1957. Many German coasters underwent similar surgery during the 1950s. She was renamed *Gaa* in 1974 and kept the name until 1988 when for a very short time she reverted to her original name before taking the name *Prima*. In 1995, she was sold to her present owner in Finland for whom she continues to trade under the name *Erika*.

(Cedric Catt)

A general view of Charles Hill and Sons Ltd's Albion Shipyard on 10 August 1976. In the Drydock is the **Harry Brown** and under construction is the **Miranda Guinness**, the last ship to be built by this yard. Berthed outside is the Port of Bristol Authority's dredger **S D Severn**, which was also built by the yard but in 1966. In the foreground, the loaded **Sand Gem** passes inbound to the Grove. At the time, she was working for the Holms Sand & Gravel Co while their 1962-built **Harry Brown** was in drydock. The **Harry Brown** was sold to owners in the Middle East in 1990 and was renamed **Alwardi 4**. She was then renamed **Sabari** in 1992, and since 1995 has worked for Bahrain-based owners as **Salaiti 17**.

(Cedric Catt)

Another view of the **Sand Gem**, this time turning in Bathurst Basin after discharging at the Holms' berth on 24 June 1976. She had recently been repainted in red oxide livery and was making an extra trip for the Holms company due to a suction pipe fault on their **Harry Brown**. Bristol General Hospital dominates the background. The **Sand Gem** was built as a conventional coaster by Philip and Sons, Dartmouth, in 1949. Initially named **Wimborne**, she traded as such until 1968 when she was renamed **Jersey Castle**. In 1970 she was sold to Sand Supplies (Western) Ltd for conversion to a sand dredger. This conversion was carried out at Saul on the Sharpness - Gloucester Canal. She was renamed **Sand Gem** for her new trade. She was too large to pass Redcliffe Bridge in order to reach the company's wharf, and so her owners obtained the lease of the depot and travelling crane at Hotwells Dock which had previously been used by Osborn and Wallis, local coal hauliers and ship owners. Sold in 1981, she was renamed **Black Gem** because her new owners intended using her to dredge sea coal. However, the necessary licence was not granted and she continued to work as a sand dredger at first in the Solent but latterly out of Padstow, eventually being demolished there in 1990.

(Cedric Catt)

The **Sand Pearl** was built by Charles Hill at Bristol as the motor barge **Wycliffe** in 1949 and converted to a sand dredger in 1967. She became the **Sand Pearl** in 1970. On 20 August 1976, she has left Renwick's Wharf and will soon be heading down the Avon to load another cargo of sand in the Bristol Channel. She is passing the **Harry Brown** at the Grove. In 1980, **Sand Pearl** left the upper reaches of the Bristol Channel after purchase by T W Grace, of Barnstaple, by whom she was renamed **Ted Grace**.

(Cedric Catt)

Berthed at Canons Marsh in the City Docks on 8 April 1977 is the **Mount Zeria**. Formerly the **Silver Cloud**, she had received attention at the Albion Dockyard (see page 16) and had just been taken over by new owners. She sailed to Antwerp the following day. The ship has had several owners and names since her construction in 1964 at the yard of Gebr van Diepen, Waterhuizen. She began life as the **Schoonbeek** and kept this name until 1974 when she took the name **Silver Cloud**. After being renamed **Mount Zeria** as noted above, it proved to be a short-lived name change for in 1978 she became **Anko** and then **Martha** in 1986 and **Mex** in 1988. It is thought that she continues to exist under the name **Diamond I** which she took in 1992. Last reported operators are listed as the Arab Tanker Services Co, so she could possibly have a limited role somewhere in the Middle East. Reverting to Bristol, the whole area of Canons Marsh is being redeveloped as part of a "bold millennium project".

(Cedric Catt)

The **Gladonia** typifies the sturdy design of coaster emanating from British shipbuilding yards during the early and mid 1960s. She was built at Goole in 1963 for J Wharton (Shipping) Ltd, a family company based on the River Trent. Sold by the Wharton company in 1985, she then suffered a rather chequered career which saw her sail to the West Indies before arriving back in the Bristol Channel for a period of lay-up in Barry during most of 1986 at which time she was named **Integrity**. Her local connections became much stronger in early 1987 when she was bought by Runwave Ltd, of Avonmouth, and she regained her previous identity of **Gladonia**. In February of that year, she crossed from Barry and sailed up the River Avon to be refurbished in the Albion Drydock, once part of Charles Hill's yard. In this view, she is about to enter Avonmouth on 7 September 1991. Her eventual fate is mysterious. She was sold to Egyptian owners in September 1994 but found herself at the centre of a dispute in the port of Setubal at the end of that year. She was arrested but slipped away and was reported at Bizerta in March 1995. Although her name has disappeared from movement reports, she seems to have survived these dramas and was renamed **Samaret Jama** under the Belize flag in 1997.

(Bernard McCall)

The dock system at Avonmouth in fact comprises four separate docks. Avonmouth Dock itself is the oldest of these. Built by a private company, it was opened in 1877 and in 1884 it was acquired, along with Portishead Dock, by the Bristol City Council. Photographed at N Berth in Avonmouth Dock on 11 July 1976 was the *Echo*, built at the Charles Hill yard in Bristol in 1957 and owned by the Bristol Steam Navigation Co Ltd. She and her fleetmates linked Bristol and ports in South Wales to Dublin and Cork in the west, and to Antwerp and Rotterdam in the east. Built as a general cargo ship, she was lengthened in 1969 and was equipped to carry containers in two of her three holds and on her upper deck hatch covers. She left the British flag when sold in 1980 and became *Ageliki III*, a name which lasted until 1983. She was then renamed *Katerina M* and later that year *Hiba*. In 1988, she was renamed *Tsambika* but again this was only a short-lived name for she became *Agion Oros* in that year and then *First Feeder* in 1989. Four years later, she took the name *Akamantis*. In 1995, she was renamed *Sea Lord* and it is under this name that she continues to trade in the Mediterranean, calling regularly at ports such as Ravenna, Limassol, Lattakia and Beirut. Now more than forty years old and having traded for a succession of owners since her move to the Mediterranean in 1980, she has proved to be a fine testament to the workmanship of her original builders.

(Cedric Catt)

Royal Portbury Dock is situated on the western side of the River Avon, opposite Avonmouth. Construction of the new dock began on 2 May 1972 and was officially opened and named by Her Majesty The Queen on 8 August 1977. It has the odd distinction of having construction started in one county - Somerset, and completed in another - Avon! This was thanks to the reorganisation of local government in the mid-1970s. Much of the traffic handled brings in large bulk carriers, vehicle carriers and other roll on/roll off vessels. Coasters are infrequent callers but the late 1990s have witnessed imports of timber from the Baltic in smaller vessels than usually seen in the dock. On 5 March 1998, the *Sagitta* was discharging 882 packages of timber from the Estonian port of Tallinn. The hull of this sturdy coaster, strengthened to carry heavy cargoes and also strengthened for ice navigation, was built at the Damen Shipyard, Bergum, and construction was completed at the company's Gorinchem yard in 1990. She was launched as *Rosemarie* but entered service under the name *Sagitta*.   (P W Hobday)

An unusual caller at Ford's grain terminal to load wheat for Dundalk on 27 December 1986 was the **Saint Brandan**, owned by J & A Gardner Ltd, of Glasgow. She was built in 1976 by J W Cook & Co, Wivenhoe, and is a multi-purpose vessel. As well as being able to carry bulk cargoes in her hold, she is fitted with a bow ramp which enables her to carry roll on/roll off cargoes. Although originally intended for working in Scotland, her multi-purpose facilities have made her an ideal ship for use in a very different part of the world. In April 1982, she was chartered by the British Government to move supplies during the Falklands campaign. She returned to Britain in mid-1984 and was replaced in the South Atlantic by her fleetmate **Saint Angus**. She returned to the Falklands in early May 1987, allowing the **Saint Angus** to return. The **Saint Brandan** has remained in the South Atlantic since that time helping to rebuild the local communities.

(Cedric Catt)

37

A colourful view of Avonmouth Dock on 28 August 1979 with the **William J Everard** discharging grain from Le Tréport at Spiller's Mill. Apart from the installation of a new engine in 1974, this coaster had a fairly conventional life after her construction at Goole in 1963. However, in 1982, she was sold by the Everard company to Wimpey Marine Limited and converted into a drilling ship named **Wimpey Geocore**. In 1988, she was converted back into a dry cargo coaster and renamed **Seaburn Girl**. There then followed a series of name changes which saw her becoming **Husum** in 1990 and then **Epson** and **Ecowas Trader** in 1992. Current owners are noted as East West Coast Marine Services, of Lagos. Apparently a geographically-challenged company!

(Cedric Catt)

From the mid-1960s, Bell Lines developed into a very successful operator of small container ships initially working across the Irish Sea but by the 1990s linking various near-Continental ports to the UK and Republic of Ireland. In late 1993, the company transferred its Bristol Channel base from its own private dock on the River Usk to Avonmouth. In this view we see the **Otto Becker** loading for Waterford on 6 December 1993, the first day of services from Avonmouth. The mid-1990s saw continued rapid expansion, possibly too rapid, for the company was beset by financial problems in 1997 and eventually ceased trading. The **Otto Becker** was built by J J Sietas in 1989 and is owned by Captain Rolf Becker.

(Bernard McCall)

A spectacular view from the top of the Spillers silo at Sharpness on 2 August 1981. The view is looking north with the River Severn in the background. The building in the centre background was originally the Sharpness Hotel, known locally as the "Shant" and is now the dock workers' social club. The red brick building behind is a disused water tower. The green coaster to the left is the Irish-flagged *Trostan* built at Goole in 1964 as the *Northgate* for trading as a small container vessel on the Irish Sea. She was sold to her Irish owners and renamed *Trostan* in 1979, and then became *Pekari* in 1981. Sold on again in 1989, she became *Elmham* and then *Tia* in 1992 when owned by Panamanian flag operators. The *Trostan* was discharging fertiliser from St Malo. The grey coaster was the German *Thor*, discharging a cargo of timber from Archangel. She was a 1965 product of the J J Sietas yard. In 1991, she was sold to Mediterranean operators and renamed *Emilie* but disappeared from movement reports in late 1992. In 1997, she was sold again and was renamed *Exodus I* but her trading routes remain uncertain.

(Cedric Catt)

Situated to the south of the entrance basin at Sharpness is an open expanse of grass from where there are excellent views down channel to the Severn bridges as well as the opportunity to see ships approaching or leaving the docks. Arriving ships turn to port off the dock entrance in order to stem the tide prior to entering the tidal basin. This manoeuvre has just been completed by the incoming *Parizhskaya Kommuna* which was bringing 2900 tonnes of bulk fertiliser from Kaliningrad on 2 September 1996. She is one of the "Sormovskiy" class of Russian vessels built for navigation on the vast Russian inland waterway system in addition to open sea trade. She was constructed at the Volodarskiy Shipyard, Rybinsk, in 1971.

(Bernard McCall)

The **Fulham** was built by W J Yarwood & Sons (1938) Ltd as the steamer **Empire Fulham** and was completed in October 1944. Although she arrived at Sharpness from Portsmouth on 2 April 1967, she was not renamed **Fulham** until 1974. She had served as a fresh water tanker for the Royal Navy. Prior to entry into commercial service, she was fitted with a "new" diesel engine which had, in fact, been removed from the tug **Severn Iris**, and she had a new pump room installed at her forward end. Here she is seen approaching the entrance lock at Sharpness on 11 October 1978, when owned by I P Langford (Shipping) Ltd. She conveyed effluent waste from a local company for disposal at sea. She was a familiar sight at Sharpness and, although this trade ceased in 1982, she remained there until 1987. Bought by Captain Peter Herbert, she left Sharpness on 17 April 1987 bound for Bideford. She left the latter port on 10 August and arrived at Garston for demolition three days later.

(Cedric Catt)

Another vessel to arrive on 2 September 1996 (see page 41) was the German ***Birgit Sabban*** which brought 2850 tonnes of cement from Santander. She lies in the outer basin of the port while the ***Parizhskaya Kommuna*** can be seen edging her way into the basin. The ***Birgit Sabban*** is a member of the successful Type 110 class vessels built by J J Sietas during the mid 1980s. Delivered on 5 November 1984, she replaced another vessel of the same name and basically similar design which had run aground off Bilbao earlier in 1984.   *(Bernard McCall)*

One of a large group of coasters managed by the Dutch Wagenborg company, based in Groningen, was the **Aurora**. She was built in 1955 by Hijlkema & Zonen, Martenshoek. On 20 January 1980, she was in Sharpness discharging 360 tons of locust beans from Amsterdam. Like many vessels, she left Sharpness to load china clay at the Cornish port of Par. She kept her original name for thirty years and it was only when sold to a Caribbean owner in 1985 that she took her second name, **Nabucodonosor**.

(Cedric Catt)

It is quite unusual to find a coaster flying the French flag, but the **Mercandian Caix** certainly did when she was photographed on 11 June 1978 after she had loaded barley for Algeria. She was built for Danish owners in 1972 at the Hüsumer Schiffswerft yard and was originally named **Lindinger Coral**. It was in 1978 that she was renamed **Mercandian Caix** but only two years later she was sold to owners in Qatar and renamed **Zarika**. *(Cedric Catt)*

The sun shines brightly on a glorious autumn day, 13 October 1981. The **Brendonia,** built at Goole in 1966 and owned at the time of the photograph by J Wharton (Shipping) Ltd, is a later sistership of the **Gladonia**, seen on page 34. She is seen approaching Sharpness at the end of her voyage from Gloucester where she had discharged a cargo of urea. She was bound across the Bristol Channel to Cardiff to load her next cargo. The vessel herself continues to work in the UK/near continent trades, her name now changed but slightly to **Brendonian** since 1984.

(Cedric Catt)

Evening departures from Sharpness, 2 April 1980. Under a dramatic sky, three vessels await their turn to sail. From left to right, the **Harostan** is taking general cargo to Apapa/Lagos; the **Gretchen Weston** is delivering another cargo of scrap to feed the voracious furnaces of Spanish steelworks; by contrast, the **Dithmarschen** is in ballast and is bound for Briton Ferry, on the River Neath, to load. The **Gretchen Weston** was built at the Bodewes Gruno yard, Foxhol, in 1974 as **Frendo Star**. She entered the fleet of Mardorf, Peach in 1976 and took the name **Gretchen Weston**. Sold in 1982, she was briefly renamed **Gretchen** before becoming **Mattun**, one of a handful of coasters flying the flag of Austria. She was renamed **Rogall** in 1985, **Nimus** in 1993 and presently trades as **Bonus**, her identity since 1995. The 1965-built **Dithmarschen**, like several other coasters in this book, was built at Germany's Hüsumer Schiffswerf. Sold in 1988, she became **Fe y Esperanza** and then **Green Moon** in 1992. The **Harostan** was built at the Bodewes shipyard, Martenshoek, in 1970 and was originally named **Eva Sif**. It was in 1979 that she took the name **Harostan** and retained this until 1988. There then followed a series of names in fairly quick succession - **Ifrane** in 1988, **Zois K** in 1989, **Thet** in 1991, and finally **Tiffany** in 1992. On 26 June 1993, she sank in the Caribbean Sea, an area where she had been trading for the previous two years.

(Cedric Catt)

A thunderstorm clears the Gloucestershire skies and a shaft of sunlight creates a dramatic rainbow as the German coaster *Claus Luhrs* approaches Cambridge Arms from Gloucester on 23 May 1979. She had discharged 750 tons of pig iron from Lübeck and was on her way to Sharpness to load scrap for Spain. Built in 1952 at the Bodewes yard in Martenshoek, she traded as *Jan Herman* until 1965. After trading as *Claus Luhrs* for twenty years, sale in 1985 resulted in her name being altered to *Claus L* and then she took a different person's name when she became *Pedro de Sula* in 1986. A renaming to *Anneliese* in 1987 suggested a change of gender! On 26 February 1989, she had to be abandoned by her crew after losing power while on a voyage from Wismar to Gunness, on the River Trent. She drifted ashore on the island of Texel and she was eventually broken up there.

(Cedric Catt)

A fine view of the Bowker and King 1969-built tankers **Bisley** and **Berkeley** at BP's Quedgeley oil terminal on 27 May 1979. Note the flags flown by each vessel which denote that they carry hazardous cargo. The **Bisley**, built at Hessle, Humberside, was sold to Greek owners in 1990 and renamed **Naoussa**. The **Berkeley** was built at Millingen, Holland, and kept this name until her sale for demolition at Bloor's Wharf, Rainham, Kent, in 1994. The other four tankers regularly seen in the canal at this time were the **Borman** and **Budleigh**, both built in Holland, and the **Blakeley** and **Bude** which were built at Appledore. The oil terminal closed in 1985 and products for the area are brought in by road. The closure and eventual demolition of this oil terminal was probably an unwise move in view of the road congestion which afflicts this area in the closing years of the twentieth century.

(Cedric Catt)

There were just two locations along the Canal between Sharpness and Gloucester where cargoes were discharged. On the previous page, we looked at Quedgeley where petroleum products were handled. At Sandfield Wharf, Saul dry bulk cargoes were handled and it is at this wharf that the **Antilope** lies on 2 June 1981. She has almost completed discharge of her cargo of 640 tons of cal mag which she had brought from the Spanish port of Pasajes. Another Dutch coaster of classic mid-1950s design, she emerged from the N V Bodewes shipyard, Martenshoek, in 1956 as the **Rifo-An**, subsequently becoming **Agnes** in 1973 and then **Antilope** in 1980. She became **Carryson** in 1982 during which year she sailed out to the West Indies. Her next change of name came in 1984 when she became **Merchant Marine**. Her later history is unclear - she had disappeared from Registers by 1990.

(Cedric Catt)

After a brief look at the two wharves on the Canal, we return to vessels progessing along its attractive waterway and we find the 1965-built Danish coaster *Arrebo* passing Fretherne Bridge on the frosty morning of 4 November 1981. She was heading for Sharpness after discharging a cargo of pig iron at Gloucester. Like many Danish coasters, she was built at the Nordsøværftet yard, Ringkøbing, and was registered at Marstal. Renamed *Lill* in 1989 and then *Lis Weber* in 1990, she left northern Europe for the Mediterranean in 1996 after being sold to Panamanian-flag operators who renamed her *Rhodos III*.

(Cedric Catt)

The earlier section of this book contains views of the shipyard of Charles Hill and Sons Ltd in Bristol and it was there that the **Colston** was built in 1955 for local owners Osborn and Wallis. Here we see her at Gloucester discharging fertiliser from Amsterdam on 18 March 1987. This was near the end of her working career in UK waters for by 13 April that year, she had been laid up at Rochester. She was then sold to West Indies operators and arrived in Barbados in January 1988. She retained her name until mid-December 1992 when she was renamed **Stengard** following a further sale. Initially placed under the flag of Honduras, she transferred to Belize registry on 1 March 1995. She remains active in the Caribbean, though she now carries a crane.

(Cedric Catt)

The **Camilla Weston** was photographed at Burrows Silos, Gloucester, on 18 November 1979. She was discharging a cargo of wheat which had been loaded at Liverpool's Royal Seaforth Dock. Clearly evident are the funnel markings of owners Mardorf, Peach and Co Ltd, of London. She was one of a pair of sisterships built in 1966 at the Boele shipyard, Bolnes, for Blue Star Line with the purpose of transhipping cargoes between continental ports and the UK. Her original name was **Crouch** and she was renamed **Camilla Weston** following purchase by Mardorf, Peach in 1971. Her end came on 15 February 1984 when she sank after being hit by a German coaster while anchored off the Norfolk coast in thick fog during a voyage from Tilbury to Leith.

(Cedric Catt)

An interesting view of Llanthony Quay in Gloucester on 28 April 1982. Cargo handling on the *River Moy* has stopped temporarily to allow a British Railways diesel shunter, No 08849, to propel grain wagons to Burrows Silos, just off the picture to the left. The *River Moy* was discharging urea from Cobh and until 1981 had been part of the East German merchant fleet under the name *Stubnitz*. Although many of that country's vessels had been built at home, this coaster was built in 1966 by Bodewes "Volharding" at Foxhol in Holland. She traded as *River Moy* for only two years, being sold to Maltese flag operators in 1983 and renamed *Crestrunner*. She was demolished by shipbreakers in Holland during the early months of 1989. *(Cedric Catt)*

The *Arklow Vale* waits at Llanthony Quay to discharge a cargo of urea from Cork on 20 April 1981. Like so many coasters in this book, she was built in Holland, this time by J Bodewes at Hoogezand in 1963. Launched as *Roscrea*, she was renamed *Torquay* in 1964 and kept that name until becoming *Arklow Vale* briefly in 1972. Later in 1972, she was renamed *Glenbrook* and reverted to *Arklow Vale* in 1977. Owned by Vale Shipping Ltd at the time of the photograph, she had a rather shady later history. A proposed renaming to *Junika* in 1982 did not materialise. In 1986, a sale within the Irish Republic flag resulted in a new name rendered as both *Goldenvale* and *Golden Vale*. Whichever it was, it did not last long for in 1987 she was sold to Tanzanian owners who renamed her *Rehema*. Shortly after this, it was reported that she was lost, but the circumstances of her loss are unknown.

(Cedric Catt)

The older of the two Severn bridges, situated upstream from the newer structure, has pedestrian walkways and cycle track unlike its modern counterpart. The walkways provide an excellent vantage point for photography - although warm sunny days are certainly recommended! On 22 June 1979, Stephenson Clarke's *Steyning* approaches the bridge heading from Sharpness to Larne with a cargo of cement clinker. The second vessel to bear this name in the fleet, she was built by Clelands at Wallsend as the *Glanton* for the Sharp Steamship Co Ltd, of Newcastle. She was purchased by Stephenson Clarke and renamed in late 1971. She left the British flag when purchased in 1981 by Panamanian flag operators who renamed her *Julia*. She was eventually sold to Turkish shipbreakers and arrived at Aliaga late in 1988. *(Cedric Catt)*

In recent years, Sharpness has continued to handle considerable quantities of cement but it has been imported in bulk from Spain. Vessels operated by Arklow Shipping have been regularly used in the late 1990s, and the **Arklow Meadow** had brought her cargo from Santander on 14 July 1998. We see her approaching the Severn Bridge three days later, on passage to Dublin to load her next cargo. She was built by J G Hitzler at Lauenburg in 1990.

(Bernard McCall)

Photographed leaving Sharpness on 19 April 1997 is the **Shetland Trader**, operated by Hay & Co, of Lerwick. She and previous vessels of this company have long been involved in the import of talc from the Baltasound. This was, in fact, her 119th visit to Sharpness and proved to be her final call for she was sold to Mediterranean owners during May and renamed **Shetland Tramp**. She was built by J Bolson & Son Ltd, of Poole, in 1972 as the **Parkesgate** for the Hull Gates Shipping Co Ltd, of Grimsby. By 1974, she was firmly established on routes which saw her carrying steel to British ports from the Hoogovens steel works at Ijmuiden. After acquisition by her Scottish owners in 1979, she began to make frequent calls to Sharpness and would sail in ballast to load stone in Cornwall for delivery to the south east of England whence she would work her way back up the east coast to her Shetland base.

(Mike Nash)

Cargoes of fish meal, usually from Iceland, have been imported to Gloucester and Sharpness for many years. The attractive Danish coaster **Lone Boye** arrives at Sharpness with such a cargo on 13 July 1998 and she was photographed as the water level in the lock was beginning to rise. The vessel was built at the Nordsøværftet yard, in Ringkøbing, in 1967 as **Else Lindinger** and had a further five names before taking the name **Lone Boye** in October 1997. She was the sixth vessel to be delivered in a very successful standard class which eventually totalled sixty-one vessels. They were built for world-wide trading although of modest dimensions. Indeed so modest were their dimensions that they have traded along the canal to Gloucester and this book illustrates two other members of the class on the canal. *(Dominic McCall)*

The entrance lock at Sharpness affords excellent views of vessels arriving at or leaving port. Here we find F T Everard's **Apricity** looking rather careworn as she arrives on 5 November 1981. She was to load a cargo of wheat for Le Havre. Built by Clelands Shipbuilding Co Ltd at Wallsend, she was sold to Carisbrooke Shipping in late 1982 and renamed **Heleen C**. She remained with Carisbrooke for almost six years but was sold by them in September 1988. During 1989 she was renamed **Ernest T** and then **Ernest 1**. At this time, she was owned by an Iranian company. Her name was changed to **Shad 1** in 1991.

(Cedric Catt)

The **Somersetbrook** was built in 1971 by Cochrane & Sons Ltd, Selby, for Comben Longstaff and Co Ltd, a company which was taken over by F T Everard and Sons Ltd, and this vessel came under Everard management in 1980. We see her here in the tidal basin at Sharpness on 2 March 1982 following the discharge of a cargo of phosphate rock from Dakar. In the following year, she was sold to Cypriot owners and renamed **Firmus**. Between 1985 and 1988, she changed hands three times for Italian owners being renamed **Sunray** in 1985 and **Depasped** in 1988. The latter name was shortened to **Sped** in 1992 and then two years later she was bought by Syrian owners and renamed **Mandarin**.

(Cedric Catt)

The third photograph in the sequence of British coasters. The *Topaz*, built at the Ailsa yard in Troon in 1962, was owned by William Robertson Ltd, of Glasgow, a company eventually taken over by Stephenson Clarke. Here, she lies at Sharpness on 26 May 1981, awaiting discharge of her cargo of "Dustapor" animal feed pellets from Ghent. In 1982, she was sold to Sutas Shipping Services, of Panama, and renamed *Sutas*, a name which she kept until 1985. In that year, she was renamed *Naz* and then became *Yios* in 1987. After a further two years, she was renamed *Panayotis* and currently is reported to be named *Amaphh Two*.

(Cedric Catt)

Two swans in search of food make their way past the **Gulf Venture** waiting to load general cargo at Century Quay, Sharpness, on 10 April 1982. At the time, she was operated by Gulf Maritime Co Ltd and was linking the UK and Ireland to West Africa. Her next port of call was Ipswich where she loaded further cargo before heading south. The **Gulf Venture** has had an interesting history. She was built as the **Baltic Venture** at the Doxford yard, Pallion, Sunderland. In late May 1980, she hoisted the Canadian flag and was renamed **Melville Venture**, a name which she kept until November of that year. She was sold and renamed **Gulf Venture** on 25 January 1981, transferring to the Cypriot flag. In 1984, she lost her series of "Venture" names when she was sold to owners in the Maldive Islands and renamed **Progress Liberty**. In July 1998, she suffered an engine room fire when off her home port of Male, and later drifted ashore. Although later sold for repairs, these had not started by October. At Spillers Silo, the Dutch coaster **Vanessa** is loading barley for Antwerp. Built in 1974 at the Bodewes yard, Hoogezand, she was sold to Carisbrooke Shipping in 1993 and was renamed **Vanessa C**.

(Cedric Catt)

The Spanish vessel **Extramar Oeste** was built at Bilbao in 1977 and her rounded lines are typical of Spanish design of that era. We see her here as she departs from Sharpness on 24 July 1979 on her regular container service to Bilbao. Span Line had introduced this service the previous year and had received excellent co-operation at the port. The same vessel was used throughout. So successful was the service that a larger vessel was chartered, the **Esther del Mar**, which unfortunately was not suitable for Sharpness. As a consequence, the service transferred to Bristol's Royal Portbury Dock in 1980. The **Extramar Oeste** was purchased by Portuguese interests in 1994 and was renamed **Eiffel Star**, with Madeira as her port of registry.

(Cedric Catt)

On the northern side of the port of Sharpness, adjacent to the entrance lock, is a drydock which has proved to be a very useful asset over the years. It is interesting to recall that in the 1960s, three companies were using the drydock - I P Langford (Shipping) Ltd., of Sharpness; F A Ashmead & Sons Ltd, of Bristol; and John Harker, of Knottingley. All had workshops around the drydock site. Bowker and King tankers have regularly been repaired and overhauled here and on 12 April 1982, this company's *Banwell*, then just three years old, occupied the drydock. This tanker is one of only a small number of seagoing vessels built at the yard of Cubow Ltd, on the River Thames at Woolwich. The Bowker and King fleet became part of Crescent Shipping in the late 1980s and this in turn was subsumed within the Hays Group. However, in 1997, Crescent Shipping re-emerged following another company deal. The *Banwell* has continued to serve her owners well, irrespective of company title.

(Cedric Catt)

The **Margreet** is a member of a very attractive class of Dutch coasters, all built in Holland for well-known Dutch owners/operators Wagenborg. Under the command of Captain G Broere, she had delivered 500 tons of pig iron for the Gloucester foundry and is seen on 18 May 1979 as she approaches Sharpness from the canal. She was heading for Par to load a cargo of china clay. This coaster was built in 1961 by Scheepswerf "Friesland", at Lemmer, as **Schieborg**. Her first name change came in 1972 when she lost her "borg" name characteristic of the Wagenborg fleet and became **Bonny**. She was renamed **Margreet** in 1976 and kept this name until 1983 when she took the name **Mrs White**. In 1987 she was renamed **Ellenaki** and then **Helena Sea** in 1989.

(Cedric Catt)

On 24 February 1979, Bowker and King's tanker **Budleigh** passes the stone tower support and remains of the swing section of the Severn railway bridge where it crossed the canal at Sharpness. This tanker often conveyed heating oil and she is heading for Swansea to load a further cargo. She was built at the H H Bodewes yard, in Millingen, in 1969 and was launched as **John T Stratford**. On entering service for tanker owners Bowker and King Ltd, she took the name **Budleigh**. Most of her work was undertaken in the Bristol Channel until the summer of 1990 when she was contracted to serve as a bunkering tanker working out of Port de Bouc, near Marseilles. It was required that she transferred to the French flag for these duties. In February 1992, she was sold to Nigerian owners based in Lagos, and was renamed **Christo** under the Nigerian flag.

(Cedric Catt)

The **Arklow River** was built for Dutch coaster owners Beck's and traded as the **Apollo I** until 1979 when she was sold to Irish owners and renamed **Arklow River**. Here she is seen approaching Cambridge Arms on 23 March 1982 after discharging a cargo of urea at Gloucester. After arrival at Sharpness, she loaded a cargo of anthracite for New Ross. She was sold later in the year to J and P Crews Co Ltd, and her master Peter Crews continued to operate her in the local trades under her new name of **Cynthia June**. In 1986, she was sold and renamed **Tora** and two years later was bought by Isle of Man shipowners Mezeron Ltd and renamed **Greeba River**. Once their working life in northern Europe is over, many coasters are bought by owners in the Mediterranean or Caribbean. In the Spring of 1997, the **Greeba River** was bought by a new owner in Newfoundland. Renamed **Placentia Sound**, fitted with a new engine and equipped with two deck cranes, she has continued to earn her keep in northern Canada, even voyaging to Greenland on occasions.

(Cedric Catt)

It will be clear that many of the 1950s-built coasters seen in these pages were the products of yards in Holland or Germany. The **Borkumriff** was built in the Hamburg shipyard of H Rancke in 1958. She remained in German ownership until 1989 when she was sold to British owners who renamed her **Oakham** and traded her under the flag of St Vincent and the Grenadines. Without change of ownership, she was renamed **Barlow** in 1991 and the **AD Astra** in the same year. In mid-1993, part of her original name was restored when she became **Borkum II.** On 19 June 1994, she arrived at Plymouth and was laid up, being then arrested in February 1995. She was soon released and sold for trading in the West Indies, arriving at Fort de France on 13 April 1995. By the time she was renamed **Femar** in 1996, she had disappeared from movement reports and may well still be involved in inter-island trading. This is a far cry from 12 April 1980 when she was photographed at Purton, bound for Gloucester with 800 tons of pig iron from Lübeck - a similar cargo to that carried by the **Claus Luhrs** on page 47. *(Cedric Catt)*

The date is 18 October 1980 and the Danish coaster *Stevnsklint* approaches Pilot Bridge on her way down the canal. She was heading for Sandfield Wharf, Saul, to discharge a cargo of fertiliser from the Spanish port of Pasajes and she had sailed up the canal to Quedgeley in order to turn. Bowker and King's tanker *Borman* can just be discerned at the Quedgeley oil terminal. The *Stevnsklint* was built at Hüsumer Schiffswerft, in north-west Germany, in 1963 and has remained under Danish ownership since that time although she has had two subsequent names. In 1981, she was renamed *Uno* and became the *Thuro* in 1991. Her current owner is Hans Peter Madsen, of Svendborg. *(Cedric Catt)*

After discharging a cargo of granite from Portugal at Gloucester, the Danish *Lizie Frem* is seen at a location known as Two Mile Bend, on the outskirts of Gloucester, as she makes her way back to Sharpness on 30 October 1980. The ninth in the standard class of sixty-one coasters built at the Danish Nordsøværftet yard (see pages 57 and 74), this vessel entered service as *Birthe Junior* in 1968. She became *Lizie Frem* in 1974 and retained the name until 1982 when it was altered to *Lizie Folmer*. In 1993, she was sold to new owners in St Georges, Grenada, and a few brush strokes resulted in her being renamed *Lizie J*. She remains active in Caribbean waters.　　　　　*(Cedric Catt)*

Yet another Dutch-built coaster, the **Lady Mary** began life in 1957 as the **Fem**, a product of the Bodewes "Volharding" yard, at Foxhol. Her first name change came in 1973 when she took the name **Tanny** and this changed to **Vartry** in 1976. The following year, she was purchased by local owners Crew & Tindale who traded her under the Panamanian flag as **Lady Mary**. She was an occasional visitor to the repair yard of R W Davies and Son Ltd, at Saul. She was photographed providing a mirror reflection in the canal at this location on 15 September 1979. Three days later, she sailed to Barry on charter to the Ministry of Defence. During her five years of local ownership, she was often involved in the transhipment of cargoes of ammunition from larger vessels anchored in Barry Roads into Barry Docks. Following her sale in 1982, her name was abbreviated to **Lady M**, and since 1991, she has traded until the flag of St Vincent and Grenadines as **Nadira P**.   (Cedric Catt)

The **Pamir II** was built at Foxhol in 1957 as the **Munte**, a name she kept until 1973. She was then renamed **Hontestroom** but only until the next year when she became **Procyon**, and she then took the name **Pamir II** in 1976. After this flurry of name changes in the mid-1970s, she retained a settled identity and here she rests at Sandfield Wharf, Saul, on 16 June 1982 after discharging a cargo of bagged and bulk calcium magnesite from Pasajes in northern Spain. While off Flamborough Head on passage to Seaham in January 1985, her engine room flooded and she had to be abandoned by her crew. She was towed to Hull and was eventually demolished there by shipbreakers later in the year.*(Cedric Catt)*

The only vessels which now trade to Gloucester are those which call at Riga Wharf, some two miles out of the city centre, to load filtration equipment manufactured by a company alongside the canal. At the time of writing, this trade accounts for only two or three arrivals per year. On 22 February 1997, the Danish coaster **Jenbo** was photographed at Riga Wharf as she loaded equipment for Ravenna. She was built at Stade in 1966 as **Alma Koppelman** for German owners, and was renamed **Jenbo** in 1985 following her sale to Danish owners. In autumn 1998, she was sold on to a company based in Gibraltar and after delivering a cargo to Jersey she left for Gibraltar on 22 October 1998. She is now used for trading round the Azores.

(Cedric Catt)

On 21 August 1995, a still and sunny day, the **Pinnau** makes her way from Riga Wharf along the tranquil waters of the canal at Frampton heading for Sharpness after loading 140 tonnes of equipment for the Spanish port of El Ferrol. As the deck cargo was 32 feet (9.75 metres) high, it was deemed necessary to build an extra, higher, wheelhouse for safe navigation and this is just visible behind the mast. This vessel was built in 1963 at the Büsumer Schiffswerft in Germany as **Rugia**, a name which she kept until 1975. From 1975 until 1983, she bore the name **Truso** and it was in 1983 that she became **Pinnau**. In late May 1997, she hoisted the Belize flag and began a new career trading in the Caribbean under the name **Evontim**.

(Nigel Jones)

The **Jentrader** is yet another product of the Nordsøværftet shipyard at Ringkøbing in Denmark. She is one of the standard class already illustrated by the **Lone Boye** on page 57 and **Lizie Frem** on page 69. She was the seventh vessel in the class and was launched as **Anna-Regil**. She was handed over to her owners on 22 February 1968. She has changed owners within Denmark on three occasions, becoming **Charles Trigon** in January 1970, **Marlin** in mid-October 1975 and then **Jentrader** on 9 August 1979. She has the distinction of being the Danish ship with the longest time charter, having been taken on charter by Elf Exploration (UK) plc in 1981 for the transport of oil-related supplies between ports in north-east Scotland and the Shetland Islands. However, before this charter began, she was photographed as she approached Gloucester on 7 April 1980. There were occasional imports to Gloucester of agricultural machinery from the Danish port of Sønderborg and it is such a cargo that she carries. She is passing Monk Meadow Dock where Bowker and King's tanker **Borman** is berthed.

(Cedric Catt)

Most of the photographs in this book were taken in good weather but navigation must continue in less than satisfactory conditions if at all possible. It has been very rare for the canal to be as badly affected by ice as can be seen in this photograph. The exact date is uncertain, but the year is 1963. The tug **Severn Iris** gives assistance to the **Sonja D**. Built as the **Dependent** in 1953 at Alphen a/d Rijn, the coaster was renamed **Sonja D** in 1956 and then was sold in 1963 to owners in Gabon who renamed her **La Paimpolaise**, with Libreville as her port of registry. As noted on page 42, the **Severn Iris** yielded her Ruston diesel engine to the **Fulham**.

(Peter White collection)

In these days of purpose-built and sophisticated container ships, it seems remarkable that a coaster such as the *Owenbawn* was used on a container service but the photograph provides clear evidence that this was indeed the case. Built in 1950 at Bruges as the *Alfonso*, she became *Lady Sanchia* in 1966 and then *Owenbawn* in 1968 following her purchase by Greenore Ferry Services Ltd. In 1969, she underwent modifications for use as a container carrying vessel and linked Sharpness to her operators' base at Greenore. She was sold in 1976 and was renamed *Alexandra K II*, and then *Lara Diana* in 1981, and *Anaam* in 1984. Our photograph shows her in the outer lock basin at Sharpness on 21 October 1970.

(Peter White)

If the **Owenbawn** was an unlikely container vessel, perhaps the **Saskia** was even more unlikely. Along with the Irish-flagged coaster **Reginald Kearon**, she was used to export Nuffield car parts from Gloucester to Dublin. A typical Dutch coaster of the 1950s, she was built at Foxhol in 1952 as the **Fivel**. She hoisted the Irish flag in 1970 before being renamed **Saskia**, a name which she retained until 1973. Then she took the name **Celtic Trader** for a short time, becoming **Marieke** until 1976. This name lasted for only two years for she became **Ana D** and after a further two year spell, she saw her final period of service named **Parada** until early 1980. In February of that year, she left Gijon to be demolished by Spanish shipbreakers at San Esteban de Pravia.

(Peter White)

The **St Anne of Alderney** discharges pig iron from Rotterdam at Llanthony Quay, Gloucester, on 10 February 1980. Built at Frederikshavn in 1963 as the **Jens Rand**, she was renamed **Juto** in 1974 and **Baltzborg** in 1977. When photographed, she had only just come into British ownership, her new owners being Hurd Deep Shipping Ltd, with Curnow Shipping Ltd as managers. In 1986, she was bought by an owner in Basseterre, St Kitts, and, with her name shortened to **St Anne** she has traded around the Caribbean since that time. *(Cedric Catt)*

Owned at the time by local maritime "entrepreneur" Fred Larkham, the **Vasa Sound** was by far the biggest vessel to sail under her own power up the river to Newnham-on-Severn where she was photographed in April 1991. The author of this book was, in fact, on board when she made the historic voyage from Avonmouth to Newnham on 14 April 1991. Built in 1963 at Goole for J Wharton (Shipping) Ltd as **Ecctonia**, she has a similar pedigree to the vessels seen on pages 34 and 45. In 1987 the **Ecctonia** was sold to Kirkwall-based Dennison Shipping Ltd by whom she was renamed **Vasa Sound**. After suffering serious damage following grounding in late 1990, it was thought that her career was over but there followed a remarkable series of events that would take a whole chapter to recount but which brought her to the Severn and then ultimately sail to Hong Kong to work as a fish carrier named **Sound**. In 1994, she was sold and renamed **Sea Lion 5**. That she has survived is a great credit to her builders and a fine compliment to the standard of British shipbuilding of that era. Like most other British shipbuilding yards, that at Goole is closed.

(Mike Nash)

It was not too difficult to select an appropriate vessel for the final page of this book. The local connections of the **Severn Side** are impeccable. She was built in 1952 by Sharpness Shipyard Ltd. and has Gloucester as her port of registry. She was built for the British Transport Commission and was to have been one of a class of six such vessels but the BTC changed its mind about the other five. Her trading life on the Bristol Channel saw her going up the Severn as far as Worcester. This photograph shows her leaving Sharpness for the last time in October 1977. She currently lies forlorn on the upper reaches of the River Medway. Although official lists show her name as two words, the stern of the ship clearly has it written as a single word. It was always intended to be a single word and the error probably occurred because other BTC vessels with "Severn" prefixes used two words.

(John Gillooly)